D0933541

INVENTIONS THAT CHANGED THE WORLD

THE WRIGHT BROTHERS

and the AIRPLANE

Louise Spilsbury

PowerKiDS
press

NEW YORK

Published in 2016 by **The Rosen Publishing Group**
29 East 21st Street, New York, NY 10010

Produced for Rosen by Calcium

Editors for Calcium: Harriet McGregor and Sarah Eason
Designers: Jessica Moon and Paul Myerscough
Picture Research: Harriet McGregor

Picture credits: Cover: Library of Congress, Prints & Photographs Division, Wright Brothers
collection, LC-DIG-ppmsc-06102 (fg, lt), LC-DIG-ppprs-00683 (fg, rt), LC-DIG-ppprs-00626
(bkgd). Insides: Dreamstime: Marcel De Grijs 8, Andrej Ildza 23, Lukaves 16; Library of
Congress: 7, 13, 16–17, 19; NASA: 18, 28; Shutterstock: Everett Historical 6, 10, 29, Patrick Foto
5, Josef Hanus 26–27, Willrow Hood 25; US Air Force: 20; Wikimedia Commons: 9, 11, 21,
Airwolfhound 22, Library of Congress/John T. Daniels 15, DefenseImagery/SSG Kaily Brown
27, Wusel007 12.

Cataloging-in-Publication Data
Spilsbury, Louise.
The Wright Brothers and the airplane / by Louise Spilsbury.
p. cm. — (Inventions that changed the world)
Includes index.
ISBN 978-1-5081-4643-8 (pbk.)
ISBN 978-1-5081-4644-5 (6-pack)
ISBN 978-1-5081-4645-2 (library binding)
1. Wright, Orville, — 1871-1948 — Juvenile literature. 2. Wright, Wilbur, — 1867-1912 —
Juvenile literature. 3. Aeronautics — United States — Biography — Juvenile literature.
I. Spilsbury, Louise. II. Title.
TL540.W7 S65 2016
629.13'0092'2—d23

Manufactured in the United States of America
CPSIA Compliance Information: Batch #BW16PK: For Further Information contact Rosen Publishing, New York, New York at 1-800-237-9932

CONTENTS

THE POWER OF FLIGHT

When Wilbur and Orville Wright made their first successful flight in an airplane that they had designed and built themselves, these now-famous brothers changed our world. Their airplane only flew for 12 seconds, but those few, short moments brought changes that still impact us today, more than 100 years later.

EARLY ATTEMPTS

Today, we take flight for granted. People regularly leave on an airplane to travel across the world for business meetings or to go on vacation. Yet, for many years, while inventors tried to develop a flying machine, people could only dream of flying. In the fifteenth century, Leonardo da Vinci came up with ideas for a helicopter and a flying machine with flapping wings, but his designs would never have flown if they had been built. In 1783, the Montgolfier brothers, who were two French inventors, built a successful hot-air balloon. Hot air is less dense than cool air, so it rises. The hot air in the large fabric balloon they made lifted a basket into the sky. The hot-air balloon carried a duck, a chicken, and a sheep into the air on their first flights!

FLYING MACHINES

Drifting in a hot-air balloon was exciting, but it did not provide the controlled, powered flight people wanted. In the 1800s, English scientist George Cayley designed a glider with wings shaped like a bird's wings. The glider was not powered, and had to be pulled along a slope to launch it. Once in the air, the shape of the wings created lift and the glider could carry a person. The glider was fun, but gliders were a little like the hang gliders people fly today. People could not fly for long in them, and could not take off and land when they chose. A true flying machine would be not be invented for some time.

Hot-air balloons were an amazing invention, but a world away from the aircraft built by the Wright brothers.

The Word Is...

Orville Wright recognized that even early people had probably longed to fly:

"The desire to fly is an idea handed down to us by our ancestors who, in their grueling travels across trackless lands in prehistoric times, looked enviously on the birds soaring freely through space, at full speed, above all obstacles, on the infinite highway of the air."

EARLY YEARS

Wilbur and Orville were the sons of Milton Wright, a church minister, and Susan Catherine Koerner Wright, who met while Milton was studying to become a minister and Susan was a student. Wilbur and Orville had two older brothers and a sister, Katharine. Wilbur was born on a farm near Millville, Indiana, in 1867, but by the time Orville was born in 1871, the family had moved to Dayton, Ohio.

GIFTED CHILDREN

From a young age, Wilbur and Orville were very close and were intrigued by the world around them. They were encouraged by their parents to explore ideas. There were many books in their home, and Susan was very practical and built interesting things for the brothers. They soon learned to make things, such as kites and woodblocks used in printing. In Dayton, the boys' father had a job editing a church newspaper, but from 1877, Milton also became a bishop and spent a long time away from home visiting his congregation. He wrote letters telling his family about the interesting places he saw and brought things back to inspire the children.

Wilbur was very smart and had an excellent memory. He was also good at sports.

WORKING TOGETHER

Wilbur missed going to college because he was injured playing hockey and spent three years recovering. He read a lot during this time, helped his father with his work, and took care of his mother who was sick.

A Flying Toy

Milton brought back a gift from one trip away that really inspired the Wright brothers' fascination with flight. It was a toy helicopter powered by a rubber band. Wilbur and Orville were intrigued by the toy and soon began to make their own versions of it, experimenting with sizes and shapes to keep it in the air longer.

Orville trained to be a printer and after their mother died, he and Wilbur opened a print store. They printed posters and other items for customers, produced two local newspapers, and designed and built first-class printing presses to sell to other printers. This first business proved they could work well as a team and showcased the technical and design skills that would lead them to new ventures.

Orville was fascinated by the world around him and was especially interested in technology and science.

BICYCLE STORE

By 1892, the Wright brothers were caught up in a new craze that was sweeping the nation: cycling. First Orville and then Wilbur bought safety bicycles, so-called because unlike the old high-wheel bicycles that had a giant front wheel and a small back wheel, the safety bicycle had two wheels of the same size. The safety bicycle was much easier and safer to ride.

A BICYCLE BUSINESS

The Wright brothers joined one of the many cycling clubs that had opened and started competing in races, too. Using their mechanical skills, they soon began repairing bikes and figured there was an opening for a new business venture. In 1892, the brothers turned the print store over to a manager and opened a bicycle sales, rental, and repair store called the Wright Cycle Exchange, in Dayton.

The big wheel at the front of the old-style bicycle made it very easy for riders to fall over the front handlebars.

BUILDING BICYCLES

Soon, in addition to selling bicycles made by other companies, the Wright brothers built bicycles to sell. They designed their own models and even developed a self-oiling bicycle wheel hub. This kept dust from the dirt streets from clogging bicycle **bearings** and causing them to wear out quickly. They also developed pedals that stayed on better, because pedals on previous bicycles often became unscrewed after a short period of use. Their experience with bicycles was to prove very useful when it came to their next project: a flying machine.

Wilbur working in the bicycle store. Only five of the bicycles the Wright brothers made still exist today.

Funding Flight

The Wright brothers made a lot of money from their bicycle business. Between 1896 and 1900, they built approximately 300 bicycles and made between $2,000 and $3,000 each per year, at a time when the average American worker earned $500 per year at most. They saved a lot of their earnings, and used them to fund their experiments in flight.

EXPERIMENTS IN FLIGHT

In 1896, a major story hit the news that attracted the Wright brothers' attention and reignited their fascination with flight. In August of that year, German inventor and pilot Otto Lilienthal died when one of the gliders he and his brother Gustav had designed fell from the air and crashed into the ground. The Wright brothers decided they would try to build a flying machine that could be better controlled.

Otto Lilienthal died tragically, but pictures of him flying his glider inspired the Wright brothers to build their aircraft.

FINDING OUT ABOUT FLIGHT

Wilbur and Orville spent the next few years finding out as much as possible about the science of flight. The brothers had learned a lot from their work designing and making bicycles from wood, wire, and metal. They knew a flying machine had to be strong but lightweight. It must be balanced and a pilot had to control it. They also knew that it had to be **aerodynamic**, which means shaped to reduce wind resistance or **drag**, and it would need an engine to stay up in the air longer.

CAREFUL RESEARCH

The brothers studied gliders and read books about George Cayley's, the Lilienthals', and other inventors' discoveries about theories of flight. They knew from existing gliders that wings should have curved tops called **aerofoils**. These produce lift when moving forward because air moves faster above than below the wing. The pressure above the wing is reduced and the wing lifts. The brothers had also observed the angles of birds' wings and feathers in flight. They used these observations to work on methods to control an airplane.

Wilbur and Orville flew their large two-winged kite to learn how to control the forces acting on an aircraft.

An Important Breakthrough

One of the brothers' first breakthroughs came in 1899, when Wilbur twisted the ends of a long, narrow box in opposite directions. The brothers built a large, two-winged kite based on this box, with fabric wings. Long ropes hung down from the two front corners of the wings, which were pulled on alternately to make the wings twist. As the kite twisted in the air, it changed direction. This system became known as "wing warping" and soon the brothers were using it to make the kite climb, dive, or turn left or right with ease.

TESTING AIRPLANES

Using the knowledge they had gathered while experimenting with their kite, Wilbur and Orville started work building their first full-sized glider. Its design was based on the kite they made but it was to be much bigger, so they used the Lilienthals' calculations to figure out how big the wings had to be to lift the machine and a pilot.

BUILDING A GLIDER

Like the kite, the brothers' glider had two wings made from a frame of light wood covered with a tightly stretched canvas. They also added a flap, known as an **elevator**, at the front. This could be angled using wires to make the nose of the glider move up or down. Pulling on other wires twisted the wing tips to make the aircraft turn left or right. Dayton was flat and usually had calm weather, so to test their glider the brothers took it to Kitty Hawk, in North Carolina, where there were few buildings, strong winds, tall sand dunes to glide from, and soft sand for landing in. Although the glider flew with a pilot on occasion, the brothers mainly flew it as a kite to help them figure out how to improve future craft.

Wilbur and Orville carried out many of their experiments in flight at Kitty Hawk in North Carolina, shown left.

Wilbur described the importance and excitement of testing and learning to ride gliders and other flying machines:

"If you are looking for perfect safety, you will do well to sit on a fence and watch the birds; but if you really wish to learn, you must mount a machine and become acquainted with its tricks by actual trial."

A TESTING TUNNEL

Between 1900 and 1902, Wilbur and Orville built and tested several glider **prototypes** with bigger and bigger wings. In 1901, the brothers built a 6-foot (1.8 m) long **wind tunnel** (which was a special kind of box with a large fan to blow air through it) on the second floor of their bicycle store. Then they set to work testing more than 200 shapes of miniature model wings in the tunnel. This allowed them to measure how the wing shapes affected the forces of lift and drag to help them find the ideal shape for flight. The brothers had to be patient because all these tests took a long time.

The brothers also tested their large, two-winged kite as a glider, with Wilbur as pilot. In this photo, he has just landed in the sand.

FIRST FLIGHT

At last, after much research and many experiments, Wilbur and Orville felt ready to attempt to build their first powered aircraft. But first, they had to find a way to power the flying machine.

A DAY TO REMEMBER

The brothers used a gasoline engine attached to a large but light wooden biplane. They were ready to make their first flight on the airplane they named the *Wright Flyer*. Their first attempts failed, then after making some repairs, on December 17, 1903, they were ready to try again. After the engine started to chug into action, it began to move across the sand. Then, suddenly and miraculously, the airplane took off. It lifted into the air and, for a few, exciting moments, it rose upward. Just as suddenly, it slowed down, stopped, and dropped safely back down onto the sand. Orville made this first successful flight, covering 120 feet (36 m) in 12 seconds.

MAKING HISTORY

The brothers took turns to make several flights that day, the longest lasting 59 seconds, allowing Wilbur to fly a distance of 852 feet (259 m) over the sand. Sadly, after the final flight, a strong gust of wind blew the *Wright Flyer* over and, as it rolled in the sand, it became badly damaged. However, Wilbur and Orville were delighted with their achievement and the small crowd watching them were amazed. The brothers had made history that day. They had succeeded in making the first powered flying machine that could take off on its own and be controlled by a pilot in the air.

On December 17, 1903, Wilbur and Orville Wright made history by successfully flying their Wright Flyer not once, but four times.

The Word Is...

Wilbur and Orville's patience and determination had paid off. As Wilbur explained:

"I am an enthusiast, but not a crank in the sense that I have some pet theories as to the proper construction of a flying machine. I wish to avail myself of all that is already known and then, if possible, add my mite to help on the future worker who will attain final success."

HOW IT WORKED

The *Wright Flyer* was a magnificent machine. To make it fly, Wilbur and Orville needed an engine, but the engines used to power cars at this time were far too heavy to attach to an airplane. So, the brothers enlisted the help of a **mechanic** at their bicycle store named Charlie Taylor. Together, they built a small but powerful gasoline engine made from aluminum, a strong but lightweight metal.

Wilbur and Orville piloted the airplane lying down because they believed it would create slightly less drag than if they were sitting up. The downside was that when the plane landed, the pilot got a mouthful of sand!

READY, STEADY, GO!

To start the engine, the pilot moved the horizontal lever with their right hand. This connected the fuel line to the engine. At the same time, assistants pulled the two **propellers** to get them spinning. Propellers have metal blades, shaped like aerofoils. When they spin, they pull the airplane forward, just like its wings lift the airplane upward. When the engine was running, the assistants let go of the wires that were holding the plane still, and it started to roll forward. As it moved through the air, the wings generated lift, pulling the plane upward, and it took off.

IN CONTROL

After working on the gliders, Wilbur and Orville added a movable **rudder** linked to the wing-warping system. To control the airplane in the air, the pilot moved the rudder and wings by pulling on the cables that were attached to them. By twisting the wings and turning the rudder lightly one way or the other, the airplane rolled left or right. By using a lever to lift the elevator flaps at the front of the plane, the pilot could move the airplane up higher or down lower in the air.

Creating Lift

When a wing moves through the air, it splits the flow of air so that half travels above the wing and half travels below it. A wing is curved so that air going over it has farther to travel. To keep up with the air flowing below the wing, the air above moves faster. This makes the air above the wing push downward less strongly. This means the pushing force on the wing from below is stronger, creating the lift needed to push the wing upward.

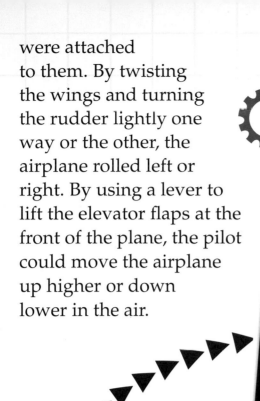

downward force

lift

air moving faster

air

wing

air moving slower

upward force

This diagram shows the cross-section of a wing with the forces acting on it as it flies. The wing lifts when the upward force is greater than the downward force.

AIRPLANES TAKE OFF!

Wilbur and Orville did not stop inventing after their historic first flight in 1903. After all, the *Wright Flyer* only flew for a short time and in one direction only. So, the brothers continued to design, build, and test more planes, producing newer and better "Flyers" each time.

THE 1904 FLYER

Wilbur and Orville knew that for their invention to be truly successful and useful, they had to make an airplane that could fly over landscapes more challenging than the windy, sandy dunes of Kitty Hawk. So, they tested *Flyer II*, which was very similar to the fatally damaged *Wright Flyer*, in 1904, at a field a few miles outside Dayton called Huffman Prairie. To this airplane they added weight to the front, to make the plane more stable, and moved the elevator farther along the wings, which made the aircraft easier to fly. On September 20, 1904, Wilbur and Orville flew their first complete circle. The flight lasted 1 minute and 36 seconds, and covered a distance of 4,080 feet (1,244 m).

Orville (left) and Wilbur (right) are shown here working on their second aircraft, *Flyer II*, at Huffman Prairie.

THE 1905 FLYER

In the fall of 1905, the Wright brothers tested their third airplane, *Flyer III*. This airplane easily stayed in the air for several minutes at a time and on October 5, Wilbur managed to circle the prairie 30 times in 39 minutes, covering a distance of 24.5 miles (39 km). Wilbur only came down to land after that time because the airplane had run out of fuel. This was it! At last, the Wright brothers were confident that they had made an airplane that was practical and could be shown to the world.

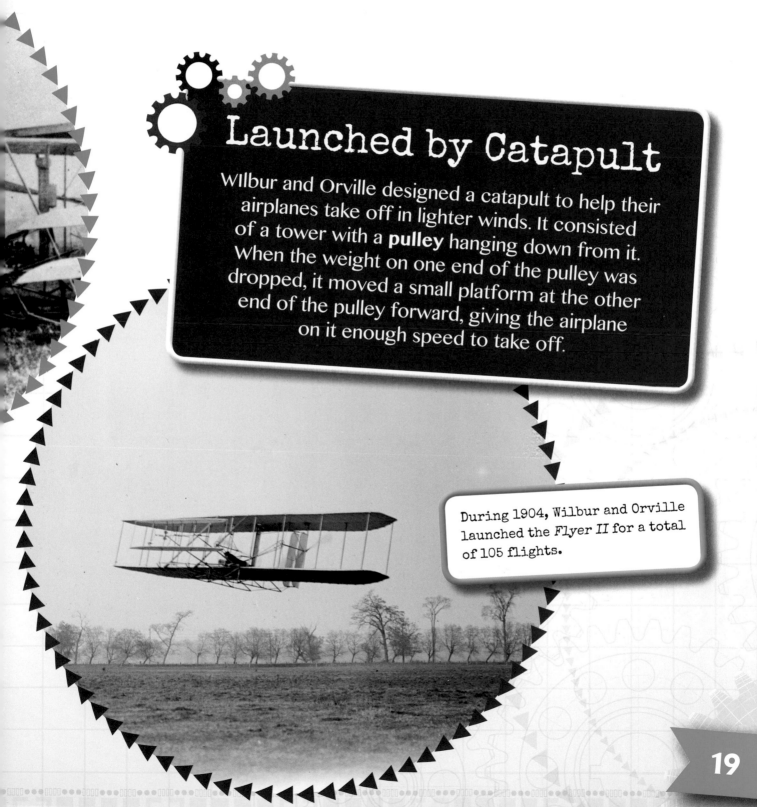

Launched by Catapult

Wilbur and Orville designed a catapult to help their airplanes take off in lighter winds. It consisted of a tower with a **pulley** hanging down from it. When the weight on one end of the pulley was dropped, it moved a small platform at the other end of the pulley forward, giving the airplane on it enough speed to take off.

During 1904, Wilbur and Orville launched the *Flyer II* for a total of 105 flights.

THE IDEA SPREADS

After flying the *Flyer III* in 1905, it was two and a half years before Wilbur and Orville piloted a plane again. During this time, they turned their attention to the business side of their work and to finding customers to buy their invention.

PATENTS AND PERFORMANCES

In 1906, the brothers took out a **patent** on their powered airplane. A patent gives an inventor ownership of an invention and ensures no one can copy it without their permission. This gave them the right to sell their invention to other companies, but first they had to persuade people that their airplane would fly. In 1907, the US Army showed interest in buying a plane, and so did companies in Europe. One way to publicize their invention was to demonstrate it in front of crowds of people, so the brothers made two airplanes and took them around the world to prove what the *Wright Flyers* could do.

Wilbur did not want to risk his airplane on a flight across water, so the first pilot to fly across the English Channel was Louis Blériot in this monoplane.

CROWD PLEASERS

In 1908, Wilbur sailed to France, where he amazed audiences with his demonstrations of the brothers' airplane. At the same time, Orville carried out demonstrations in Washington D.C. During the summer and fall of 1909, Orville carried out flight displays in Germany. In total, he made 19 flights and set world records for **altitude** (height) and flight length in front of stunned crowds of up to 200,000 people. By this time, the brothers could even take a passenger in the airplane.

Orville Wright in Berlin, Germany, in 1909, with the airplane known as the *Wright Model A*, an improved version of the 1905 Flyer.

The Word Is...

Wilbur described his excitement at discovering the joys of being a pilot:

"More than anything else the sensation is one of perfect peace mingled with an excitement that strains every nerve to the utmost, if you can conceive of such a combination."

WAR IN THE AIR

Wilbur and Orville may have begun talking to the US Army about buying their airplanes in 1905, but it was not until four years later that a deal was made. Understandably, the US Army was cautious about ensuring Wilbur and Orville's flying machine was practical and safe.

ARMY TRIALS

By 1907, the brothers had successfully sold their airplanes to companies in Europe. So, when the US War Department announced they were offering $25,000 for a flying machine that could pass certain tests, Wilbur and Orville knew they were the only inventors who could win. While Wilbur was in France demonstrating the *Wright Flyer*, Orville stayed in Dayton to work on designs for the army plane. In August and September 1908, Orville demonstrated this new plane to the US Army at Fort Myer, Virginia, a military station just outside Washington, D.C. Unfortunately, while on a trial run, a propeller broke when Orville and his passenger, Lieutenant Thomas E. Selfridge, were flying. The plane crashed, killing Selfridge and badly injuring Orville. Orville was very upset by Thomas' death and made sure that blades on future propellers were reinforced to make them much safer.

The Sopwith F.1 Camel (left) and the Fokker DR1 (right) are two of the most famous World War I (1914–1918) aircraft.

THE FIRST MILITARY AIRPLANE

Orville was not well enough to fly until July 1909, but fortunately the army had decided that even though it had crashed, the Wright brothers' plane could work. When Orville carried out more test flights in 1909, the plane passed all the army's tests with flying colors. It carried a passenger for at least 125 miles (200 km) at a speed of 40 miles per hour (64 kph) and stayed in the air for over one hour. The plane proved that it was easy to transport, easy to control and steer in all directions, and that it could land safely. It became the world's very first military aircraft.

The *B-17 Flying Fortress* is a four-engine heavy bomber aircraft developed in the 1930s for the US Army Air Corps.

Weapons of War

Airplanes were used in battle during World War I. At first they were used to spot enemies on the ground. Later fighter planes had machine guns attached to them, to shoot down enemy planes. By World War II (1939–1945), airplanes had several engines so they could carry heavy bombs long distances, and fighter planes became a vital weapon of war.

FAME AND RETIREMENT

Wilbur and Orville became famous and their pictures appeared in newspapers and magazines throughout the world. For a while, the brothers were the center of attention wherever they went.

MEETING ADMIRERS

Between 1908 and 1909, while the brothers were demonstrating their invention in Europe, they met many famous people, including political leaders and kings and queens. The brothers met King Edward VII of England. They discussed flying with King Alfonso XIII of Spain. In Germany, Orville and his sister Katharine, who traveled with him, dined with the emperor, Kaiser Wilhelm, in his castle. When they returned from Europe, a grand welcome met them in their hometown in a two-day celebration that included parades, concerts, parties, and fireworks. The brothers were presented with medals from the US Congress, the state, and the city. Schoolchildren wearing red, white, and blue stood in the shape of a flag and closed the ceremony with a song.

LATER YEARS

In 1910, Wilbur and Orville set up the Wright Company and began to make and sell airplanes. Wilbur also spent a lot of time working on **lawsuits** against people he felt had used their invention, or aspects of it, without their permission. He strongly felt that this was unfair and the stress, combined with the hours of paperwork, wore him out. In April 1912, he caught typhoid fever and he died on May 30, at just 45 years old. Orville sold the company and retired from the airplane business in 1915, three years after Wilbur's death. However, his interest in flight never ended. He worked as a **consultant** for many airplane companies and research groups. He received more medals and honors, and lived a fruitful life until he died of a heart attack in 1948, at the age of 76.

Statues and memorials have been built in many of the places where the Wright brothers flew. This is the Wright Brothers National Memorial at Kill Devil Hills, North Carolina.

WILBUR
WRIGHT
ORVILLE
WRIGHT

...OLUTION AND UNCONQUERABLE FAITH IN COMMEMORATION OF THE CONQUEST OF THE AIR

Flying High

In October 1909, Wilbur flew over New York City as part of the Hudson-Fulton celebrations to commemorate explorer Henry Hudson and inventor Robert Fulton. Fearing a crash landing in the Hudson River, he bought and attached a bright red canoe beneath the lower wing, to help him float in case the worst happened! Almost 1 million people witnessed him fly around the Statue of Liberty. They cheered wildly and people in cars and boats tooted their horns.

CHANGING THE WORLD

After Wilbur and Orville invented the airplane, the world was never the same again. The ability to fly changed the way wars were fought and enabled people to travel farther and faster than ever before.

DEVELOPMENTS IN FLIGHT

As other inventors and designers started to improve and adapt the Wright brothers' early airplanes, they became used in different ways. In 1927, Charles Lindbergh flew across the Atlantic Ocean and in 1932, Amelia Earhart became the first woman to make a transatlantic flight alone. In 1935, the *Douglas DC3* carried 24 passengers and became the first passenger airplane to make a profit. By the 1950s, airliners could carry about 100 passengers at a time. In 1970, the jumbo jet carried its first passengers. The invention of the jet engine meant planes could fly higher and farther than ever before. By 1976, famous **supersonic** jet *Concorde* took passengers from New York City to Paris in just four hours!

BRINGING PEOPLE TOGETHER

Today, people are inventing airplanes powered by the sun's energy and looking at designs for space airplanes that could carry ordinary people to the

Today, airplanes are in the world's skies every minute of every day, taking off and landing from large, busy airports like this one in Canada.

moon and back. Flying has not only changed the way people travel, being able to fly has brought people around the world closer. People can do business with different countries and because we can visit foreign countries, we also learn and understand more about different ways of life. Wilbur and Orville could never have known what an impact their invention would have on our world.

Wilbur and Orville developed powered flight, making possible the vital role aircraft play in the armed forces today.

The Word Is...

Wilbur and Orville had dared to dream that they could fly when many believed it was impossible. They could not predict what would result from their own invention, with Orville mistakenly stating:

"No flying machine will ever fly from New York to Paris . . . [because] no known motor can run at the requisite speed for four days without stopping."

TIMELINE

1783 The Montgolfier brothers of France make the first successful flight in a hot-air balloon.

1804 George Cayley builds a single-winged glider.

1809 George Cayley publishes a book that explains important facts about flight, such as how the shape of a wing can generate lift.

1853 George Cayley makes the first-ever successful glider flight carrying a person.

The *Flyer II* is shown here being moved out of the storage hangar that Wilbur and Orville built on the prairie.

1867 Wilbur Wright is born in Millville, Indiana.

1871 Orville Wright is born in Dayton, Ohio.

1891 German inventor Otto Lilienthal becomes the first person to make several flights in a glider.

1892 Wilbur and Orville open a bicycle sales, rental, and repairs store called the Wright Cycle Exchange, in Dayton.

1896 One of Otto Lilienthal's gliders crashes and he is killed.

1899 Wilbur and Orville build their biplane style kite.

1903 Wilbur and Orville make the first flight in the *Wright Flyer*.

1908 Wilbur and Orville start to make and sell airplanes.

1909 Louis Blériot's single-winged airplane the *Blériot XI* makes the first crossing of the English Channel.

1919 British pilots John Alcock and Arthur Brown make the first nonstop flight across the Atlantic Ocean.

1927 Charles Lindbergh makes the first transatlantic solo flight.

1928 The world's first air ambulance service is set up to carry people to the hospital by airplane in emergencies and from remote places.

1932 Amelia Earhart becomes the first woman to fly across the Atlantic Ocean alone.

1935 The *Douglas DC3* becomes the first plane able to make money just by carrying passengers.

1939 The German *Heinkel He 178* becomes the first airplane to fly with a jet engine.

1947 US Air Force pilot, Chuck Yeager, flies faster than the speed of sound in the world's first supersonic flight in the airplane *Bell X-1*.

1960S The Harrier jump jet is designed. It can fly straight upward at takeoff by aiming the jet engines on its sides downward.

1961 Russian astronaut, Yuri Gagarin, becomes the first person in space.

1969 US astronauts Neil Armstrong and Edwin (Buzz) Aldrin, Jr., become the first to walk on the moon.

1970 The first jumbo jet, the *Boeing 747*, carrying 153 fare-paying customers, enters service.

1976 *Concorde* is the first supersonic jet to operate a passenger service, traveling from New York City to Paris in just four hours, half the time it takes a jet to fly the same distance.

1989 Stealth bombers, airplanes designed to be invisible to enemy radar systems, take their first flight.

Otto Lilienthal flying his two-surface glider in the early 1890s.

2000 The first crew start work in the International Space Station (ISS).

2003 The first test flight of *Helios*, a solar-powered plane, ends in disaster when the plane breaks up and falls into the Pacific Ocean.

2004 *SpaceShipOne* becomes the world's first private airplane to fly to the edge of space.

2005 The first superjumbo, the *Airbus A380*, is launched and becomes the world's largest passenger plane. It is designed to carry 555 passengers.

2010 *HB-SIA* becomes the first solar-powered aircraft capable of flying at both day and night.

2014 *SpaceShipTwo*, a spacecraft designed to take tourists on short trips to space in the future, makes its first test flight.

GLOSSARY

aerodynamic Shaped to reduce the drag from air moving past.

aerofoils Curve-shaped parts of an airplane's wing that help it fly.

altitude The height of an object in the sky in relation to sea level.

bearings Parts that reduce the friction between important moving parts inside a machine.

consultant A person who gives expert advice on a subject.

drag Force of air that pushes against objects. Drag slows down planes in the sky.

elevator A hinged flap on the tail plane of an aircraft.

lawsuits Processes in which courts make decisions to end disagreements between people.

mechanic A person who repairs machines.

patent A document issued to someone who invents something new so that other people do not copy it without permission.

propellers Devices with two or more metal blades that turn quickly. Propellers make ships and planes move forward.

prototypes First or early models of new inventions or designs.

pulley A wheel or set of wheels used with a rope or chain to lift or lower heavy objects.

rudder A flat blade at the back of an airplane. Moving a rudder right and left turns the airplane left and right.

supersonic Faster than the speed of sound. Supersonic planes fly faster than the speed of sound.

wind tunnel A tunnel or long box used to study the effects of air moving past solid objects.

Books

Buckley, James. *The Wright Brothers* (Who Were). New York, NY: Grosset & Dunlap, 2014.

Dunn, Joe. *The Wright Brothers* (Bio-Graphics). Minneapolis, MN: ABDO Publishing, 2007.

Mellett, Peter, and John Rostron. *What is Flight?: Birds, Planes, Kites, Balloons* (Exploring Science). Helotes, TX: Armadillo, 2015.

Robinson Masters, Nancy. *Airplanes* (21st Century Skills Innovation Library: Innovation in Transportation). North Mankato, MN: Cherry Lake Publishing, 2013.

Santella, Andrew. *The Wright Brothers: Inventors and Aviators* (Our People). North Mankato, MN: The Child's World, Inc., 2014.

Venezia, Mike. *The Wright Brothers: Inventors Whose Ideas Really Took Flight* (Getting to Know the World's Greatest Inventors and Scientists). New York, NY: Childrens' Press, 2010.

Websites

Due to the changing nature of Internet links, PowerKids Press has developed an online list of websites related to the subject of this book. This site is updated regularly. Please use this link to access the list: **www.powerkidslinks.com/itctw/wright**

INDEX